HE SAYS/SHE SAYS

By Marnie Winston-Macauley
and
Cindy Garner

ANDREWS AND MCMEEL
A Universal Press Syndicate Company
Kansas City

To Ian, Simon, Terry –and Joshua,
the men in my life who think exactly as I do
and never, ever "misunderstand" me.

ℰℕ

Library of Congress Catalog Card Number: 95-77557

ISBN: 0-8362-0558-8

ATMOSPHERE

SHE: Any place with romantic surroundings, such as tables for two, candlelight, a harpist, or a strolling violinist.

HE: *Any place with free pretzels and a large screen showing "Monday Night Football."*

BEST FRIEND

SHE: A proven chum you can count on with your life to keep your confidences and help out in an emergency.

HE: *Any guy at the bar who will lie for you.*

CHALLENGE

$\mathcal{S}$HE: *Succeeding in a tough new job so you can help support your family.*

HE: **Swallowing the worm at the bottom of your bottle of tequila.**

❧

Communing With Nature

SHE: *Establishing an intimate connection with the land, its plants, and animals.*

HE: **Walking into the bushes for a quick pee.**

&

COMPATIBILITY

SHE: *The feeling of being "right" together that only gets better over time.*

HE: **A feeling you had until your honeymoon, then can only seem to find with everyone but your wife.**

ↁ

Conversational Topics

SHE: Interesting people, world affairs, social problems.

HE: *Football.*

Courting

SHE: That delightful initial period of romance when couples pay special attention to each other, with lots of kisses, flowers, and tender words.

HE: *That time during which you do what it takes to get her into the sack . . . after which you can go back to being yourself.*

CRISIS

SHE: *A serious problem requiring immediate, intelligent action, e.g., a pipe bursts, the stove catches on fire.*

HE: **You're down to your last Bud.**

&

DANCING

SHE: A pleasurable musical activity, often a sensual prelude to sexual intimacy.

HE: **Something you do with every woman in the room except your own.**

DAYDREAMING

SHE: Capturing idle moments by picturing you and your man playing at the beach, dancing under the stars.

HE: **Something you do while your partner's having a serious talk with you.**

DELEGATION

SHE: *Asking others to do things for the benefit of the whole family.*

HE: **Asking your wife to find your car keys, your glasses, and the remote control.**

❧

DINING OUT

SHE: Stepping out on the town to sample some gourmet feasts.

HE: *What you do with your mistress every time you see her and with your wife on her birthday.*

DINNER CONVERSATION

SHE: A lively chat about the day's events and future plans.

HE: *"What's on TV?"*

DIRECTIONS

SHE: *The first thing you ask for to make sure you find your way.*

HE: **The last thing you would ever ask for, even if you found yourself driving into a swamp.**

એ

DIVORCE (GROUNDS FOR)

SHE: Your husband is cheating on you, has a drinking problem, or a gambling problem.

HE: *Your wife keeps using your razor.*

DRESSING UP

SHE: Spending hours at the hairdresser, putting on a dynamite outfit, and making sure your makeup is perfect.

HE: *Changing your socks.*

DOCUMENTARIES (MUST SEE)

SHE: *The Making of a President*

HE: **The Making of a Centerfold**

ECSTASY

SHE: The height of passionate pleasure, e.g., a satisfying sexual encounter with your husband, hearing a magnificent piece of music.

HE: *Having the remote control in one hand and a beer in the other.*

EXERCISE

SHE: A rigorous workout that tones and strengthens your muscles and cardiovascular system, such as jogging, bicycling, and aerobic dancing.

HE: *Moving from the dinner table to the couch.*

ETIQUETTE (IN AUTOMOBILES)

SHE: *Thanking him for opening your door first.*

HE: **Remembering to roll down the window before you spit.**

ᘓ

FAITHFULNESS

SHE: Loyalty that lasts through a lifetime.

HE: *Loyalty that lasts through your wedding night.*

FATHER/SON TALK

SHE: A chance to pass on useful information every boy needs to know.

HE: *A chance to teach him how to belch and break enough wind to put out a lit match.*

FATHERLY ADVICE (TO TEENS)

SHE: *Telling them you care, then guiding them with love and wisdom.*

HE: **Telling them to talk to their mother.**

❧

Favorite Women's Sports

SHE: Ice skating, tennis.
HE: *Mud wrestling, nude volleyball.*

Fidelity

SHE: Being true to your loved one.
HE: *A leading family of mutual funds.*

FIRST DATE

SHE: *A chance to get to know someone new and possibly make a new friend. Recommended plans: a quiet dinner followed by a walk, during which you can leisurely explore common interests.*

HE: **A "fresh meat" opportunity. The chance to get as far as you can as fast as you can.**

FIRST DATE FOLLOW-UP

SHE: Calling to thank him; dropping him a sweet note.

HE: *Calling her in a month or two . . . if you can find the matchbook cover you wrote her number on.*

FLAVOR ENHANCERS

SHE: Fancy herbs like ginger, tarragon, thyme, nutmeg, and basil.

HE: *Mustard and ketchup.*

FOREIGN TRAVEL

SHE: *A romantic exploration of exotic spots, e.g., a luxury cruise to Antigua aboard the Royal Odyssey, a tour of the French wine country.*

HE: **Driving down to Tijuana for "Happy Hour."**

☙

FOREPLAY

SHE: Prolonged erotic stimulation characterized by mounting sexual excitement.

HE: *Twenty seconds of kissing.*

GARAGE

SHE: A place to park the car.

HE: *A place to tinker with hammers, nails, and screws for hours . . . without ever actually fixing anything.*

GIFT (FROM EUROPE)

SHE: An oil painting of Notre Dame Cathedral by an artist on the Left Bank.

HE: A "Kiss Me If You're French" T-shirt from the duty-free shop at the airport.

∽

GOOD JOKE

SHE: A funny story with a witty, surprise punch line.

HE: *A funny story you tell over and over and over every time anyone comes over.*

GOURMET MEAL

SHE: Fine fare, pleasingly presented, often taking hours to prepare, e.g., vichyssoise, fois gras, escargots, and a bottle of Pouilly-Fuissé.

HE: *A hot dog with French's mustard and a bottle of imported beer.*

GULLIBLE

SHE: *Too willing to believe.*

HE: Your wife when you tell her: "The traffic was backed up for two hours" or "I only read *Playboy* for the articles."

❧

HAIRDO (FLATTERING)

SHE: Getting just the right cut and color to suit you.

HE: *Growing one hair long enough to circle your bald spot like linguine.*

HEROINES

SHE: Mother Teresa, Joan of Arc, Florence Nightingale.

HE: *The Dallas Cowboy cheerleaders.*

HONESTY

SHE: *Sharing your deepest thoughts and feelings.*

HE: **Telling your real first name on a date.**

ആ

Illness

SHE: A sickness serious enough to put you to bed, like a fever of over 102°.

HE: *A paper cut.*

Illogical

SHE: Irrational.

HE: *Any woman who disagrees with you.*

In-Depth Conversation

SHE: *A thorough talk that allows you to express your feelings honestly and completely.*

HE: **One that lasts during the entire halftime.**

ൟ

INDIVIDUALITY

SHE: Your unique personal style, e.g., letting your hair grow and braiding it intricately around your head.

HE: Letting the hair in your ears sprout like Brillo pads.

INNER STRENGTH

SHE: The ability to cope with life's great challenges.

HE: The ability to twist the cap off a beer bottle with your teeth.

INTIMATE CONVERSATION
(WITH SAME-SEX PALS)

SHE: *Sharing your innermost feelings about the world around you.*

HE: **Sharing your innermost feelings about who you'd like to make it with while drinking beer and watching strippers.**

℘

JEALOUSY

SHE: Anger brought on by envy and fear of losing a loved one.

HE: *Demanding to know everything your wife did while you were out with your girlfriend.*

JUMPING TO CONCLUSIONS

SHE: An incorrect assumption based on faulty facts.

HE: *When your wife assumes you've been fooling around just because there's lipstick on your T-shirt and you smell like perfume.*

KISSING

SHE: *With someone new, an expression of enjoyment or attraction.*

HE: **First base.**

ఌ

LISTENING

SHE: Focusing exclusively on what he has to say.

HE: *Paying attention until you think of something more important to say, at which time you cut her off.*

LITERATURE

SHE: The classics. Any work that has enduring artistic value, e.g., *Julius Caesar* and *Romeo and Juliet* by Shakespeare.

HE: **Playboy,** *the swimsuit edition of* **Sports Illustrated.**

Logic

SHE: *Using your brain to draw intelligent conclusions.*

HE: **Pushing an elevator button a hundred times so it will get there faster.**

❧

MAIL (IMPORTANT)

SHE: Correspondence vital to your daily life. The electric bill, your child's report card.

HE: *Your copy of* Penthouse, *anything from Ed McMahon.*

MANNERS

SHE: Courtesy. Formal and informal rules of thoughtful behavior designed to make others in your presence feel comfortable and appreciated, e.g., sending "Thank You" notes, helping the elderly across the street.

HE: *1. Wiping your mouth after you take a swig from the milk carton.*
2. Holding the door open while your wife lugs in the groceries.

Manners (For Company)

SHE: *Waiting to do the dishes until after they leave.*

HE: **Waiting to fall asleep until after they leave.**

☙

MATURE WOMAN

SHE: One who has grown older with grace and dignity.

HE: *A broad who's over the hill.*

MINOR DETAILS

SHE: Unimportant facts you sometimes neglect to mention, e.g., the paper arrived ten minutes late this morning.

HE: *Forgetting to tell your girlfriend you're married.*

MONOGAMY

SHE: *Being honest and true to one man.*

HE: **All your girlfriends only date you.**

ↁ

Mourning Period (For a Spouse)

SHE: At least a year.

HE: *Waiting at least till your wife's in intensive care before venturing out to the local singles bar.*

Neatness Freak

SHE: Orderliness, putting everything in its proper place.

HE: *Shoving your toenail clippings to one side of the bathroom floor.*

Nightmare (Worst)

SHE: *Nuclear war breaks out; a loved one has an incurable disease.*

HE: **The Super Bowl is preempted by *As the World Turns*.**

❧

Night on the Town

SHE: A festive dinner followed by dancing to a live band or the viewing of a first-run movie.

HE: *Barhopping.*

Old Back Injury

SHE: Something you ignore so you can get on with your work.

HE: *Something you complain about constantly so you can get out of doing any work.*

PASSION

SHE: *Intense feeling of love and longing for another person.*

HE: **What gets you to the altar and then magically disappears after the honeymoon.**

❧

Pastimes (Interesting)

SHE: Reading a good book, playing a board game, conversing.

HE: *Scratching your crotch, spitting.*

Paying Attention

SHE: Listening and responding with interest to another person.

HE: *Saying "uh-huh" before turning on the TV.*

PILLOW TALK

SHE: *Exchanging words of love that describe the sensual experience you've both just shared.*

HE: **Saying, "Tell the truth, babe . . . was I great, or what?"**

&

Planning for the Future

SHE: Thinking through problems and opportunities to ensure that the days ahead are comfortable and secure for your family.

HE: *Buying a six-pack for the weekend.*

Promise

SHE: A sincere pledge you wouldn't break except in the case of death or a natural disaster.

HE: *Anything you can come up with at the moment to get her into bed.*

QUALITY TIME

SHE: *Time spent with people you love, sharing activities you all enjoy.*

HE: **Time spent with your buddies watching football, while your wife and kids lug in your beer.**

☙

RECYCLING

SHE: Preserving nature's precious resources by returning them to their original state.

HE: *Reusing beer cans as ash trays. Turning over your girlfriend to your best buddy when you're bored with her.*

REFRIGERATOR (STOCKED)

SHE: A week's supply of dairy, meat, fruit, and vegetables to provide for your own needs and those of drop-in guests.

HE: *A six-pack, a frozen pizza, and a pint of Haägen-Dazs.*

RESPECTING DIFFERENCES

SHE: *Honoring the desires and thoughts that divide you.*

HE: **Not caring what she drinks, so long as she has plenty of beer at home for you.**

೫

Romantic Hideaway

SHE: A charming country inn; a ski lodge in the mountains.

HE: Motel 6.

Satisfaction

SHE: The feeling you get from having your husband and children happy and content.

HE: The feeling you get from drinking your best buddies under the table.

Scent (Intoxicating)

SHE: *Any aroma that evokes a pleasurable or sensual response, often associated with a positive emotional experience, e.g., lavender, musk.*

HE: **Any smell reminiscent of beer, a new car, or a fresh lube job.**

ം

SENSITIVITY

SHE: Showing care and concern for your spouse's feelings.

HE: *Remembering not to call out your mistress's name while making it with your wife.*

SEX

SHE: The physical expression of profound intimacy between two people who have a strong and loving spiritual and emotional bond.

HE: *Scoring.*

Sexual Fantasies

SHE: *You and your lover are alone on a deserted tropical isle. He patiently kisses each and every part of you, you make passionate love for hours. Then he tenderly holds you till the sunlight streams across your naked bodies.*

HE: **Anything with three women and whipped cream.**

SEXUAL REFERENCE BOOK

SHE: *The Joy of Sex*

HE: **The Happy Hooker**

SHARING RESPONSIBILITY

SHE: Both partners contributing to achieve mutual good and for the betterment of the relationship.

HE: *You leave laundry around, she picks it up; you mess up the kitchen, she does the dishes; you track in dirt, she scrubs the floor.*

STAYING POWER

SHE: *The ability to endure and carry on in the face of great challenges.*

HE: **The ability to make love to your wife for a full three minutes during the Super Bowl.**

෨ෟ

SUBJECTS THAT EXCITE YOUR MIND

SHE: Human cloning; how to save the planet; new recycling methods.

HE: What it would be like to do it with The Doublemint Twins.

SUCCESSFUL WOMAN

SHE: A woman who's climbed up the ladder through diligence and hard work.

HE: A ball-breaker.

"SWM"

SHE: *An abbreviation for Single White Male in a personal ad.*

HE: **"Sneaking While Married."**

ॐ

TELEPHONE CALL-WAITING

SHE: A telephone service that allows you to interrupt an unimportant conversation to take an important call, e.g., from your doctor or husband.

HE: *What you put your wife on when your girlfriend or buddies want to talk to you.*

THOUGHTFUL GIFTS (FOR YOUR WIFE)

SHE: Satin lingerie, a gold necklace.

HE: *A Thighmaster, a pot, a new toaster.*

"TILL DEATH DO US PART"

SHE: *We shall always be together.*

HE: **Until someone better comes along.**

❦

VIRGINITY

SHE: Sexual purity.

HE: *What you hate in the women you date, but demand in a woman on her wedding night.*

WEDDING RING

SHE: A symbol of the love you and your husband have pledged to each other.

HE: *The first thing that comes off in a singles bar.*

WORK OF ART

*S*HE: *Any object that stirs you to passion: an impressionistic painting by van Gogh or a sculpture by Rodin.*

HE: **Your neighbor in a string bikini.**

☙